ARMOR
UP

ARMOR
UP

JOHN BYTHEWAY

LAUREL CHRISTENSEN

JOHN HILTON III

HANK SMITH

ANTHONY SWEAT

BRAD WILCOX

DESERET
BOOK

Salt Lake City, Utah

To E. B. Stevens—thank you
for inspiring us and so many others.

Library of Congress Cataloging-in-Publication Data

Armor up / John Bytheway, Laurel Christensen, John Hilton III, Hank Smith, Anthony Sweat, Brad Wilcox.

    pages cm

  Includes bibliographical references.

  Summary: Six youth authors explain their take on the armor of God metaphor from Ephesians.

  ISBN 978-1-60907-317-6 (paperbound)

1. Mormon youth—Conduct of life. 2. The Church of Jesus Christ of Latter-day Saints—Doctrines. 3. Mormon youth—Religious life. 4. Mormon Church—Doctrines. I. Bytheway, John, 1962– II. Christensen, Laurel. III. Hilton, John, III. IV. Smith, Hank, 1980– V. Sweat, Anthony. VI. Wilcox, Brad.

  BX8643.Y6A68 2013

  248.8'30882893—dc23   2012041709

Printed in the United States of America

R. R. Donnelley, Crawfordsville, IN

10 9 8 7 6 5 4 3 2 1

CONTENTS

INTRODUCTION

How badly do you want to become great? If you are the type of person who likes to take on a challenge, this book is for you. As you read, you are going to be presented with the chance to make lifelong commitments, asked to make difficult changes, and invited to challenge yourself. Be warned, some of those challenges may not be easy. However, we promise that if you act on what you read in this book you will become a much more confident, happy, and successful person.

Like a knight in the Middle Ages, you face danger on a daily basis. A wise knight knew that without superior armor he could easily be killed in a dangerous world. His armor was heavy and wasn't comfortable, but he never went to battle without it. When he put it on, he took the time to fasten each piece correctly, no matter how long it took. He never shrugged and left it behind for the day, because he knew that just one day without armor could be his last. A knight knew every inch of his armor well because he inspected it often. If he noticed a piece wearing down or broken in some way, he always took the time to fix it. If the repair required skill beyond his ability, he took it to someone who could help him. This is the type of knight who survived the most brutal battles. This is the type of knight who lived to tell his children and grandchildren of his past adventures.

You face battles as well. As the Apostle Paul said, "We wrestle not against flesh and blood, but against . . . spiritual wickedness" (Ephesians 6:12). We asked some teenagers to tell us about the spiritual battles in their daily lives. Here are some of their comments:

- "Daily life is a battle. My standards are constantly being attacked and questioned by the media."
- "Satan is constantly finding ways to try and tear you down. He wants us to believe we aren't good enough. That is a lie."
- "Every day we are assaulted by the evils of the world and things are getting worse. We must fight to maintain our purity."

In a modern revelation the Lord said, "Take upon you my whole armor that ye may be able to withstand the evil day, having done all, that ye may be able to stand" (D&C 27:15). We asked these same teenagers how they felt about the armor of God. Take a look at what they said:

- "The armor of God contains the aspects of the gospel that help you remember what to work on daily. When I remembered this, I was able to overcome a horrible addiction to pornography."
- "High school is a war zone, but it doesn't have to be intimidating as long as you are allowing Heavenly Father to protect you."
- "Satan has had thousands of years of tempting others. The armor of God is the way to stand against that."
- "Wearing the armor of God can be difficult and, like real armor, occasionally feels uncomfortable. It is worth it! Besides, people wearing armor look awesome!"

One young woman who recently graduated from high school said, "I've seen in my life how important it is to put on the armor of God and keep it on. I couldn't see it then, but as I grew up and chose the right and kept the commandments, I began to see the happiness and blessings that filled my life. Through discouragement and trials, I knew the only thing that would protect me and truly bring me happiness was the strength offered to me by my Savior. Choosing to wear the armor of God and keeping it on was the best and most important decision I ever made."

In the next six chapters you are going to learn about each piece of the armor of God. Each chapter will explain why that piece of armor is important and what you need to do to make sure you have it securely fastened. Every piece is important; we can't leave any of them behind. The Apostle Paul wrote that we must put on the *whole* armor of God. As you faithfully wear this armor you will thrive spiritually and one day help your children and grandchildren shape their own armor.

If you want to line up on the Lord's side of the line, if you are ready to become the person the Lord wants you to become, then what are you waiting for? Turn the page and come with us as we *Armor Up!*

Continue the Conversation . . .

Remember the Knights of the Round Table in the story of King Arthur? The authors of this book have created a similar gathering place. You can find it at seek.deseretbook.com /armorup. Click on Roundtable Discussions and you can follow the authors' roundtable discussions for each chapter.

At seek.deseretbook.com/armorup, click on Roundtable Discussions to follow the authors' roundtable discussions for each chapter.

CHAPTER ONE

GIRT ABOUT WITH TRUTH

"Stand therefore, having your loins girt about with truth" (Ephesians 6:14)

BRAD WILCOX

Jesus—He loves me. Satan—he loves me not! No doubt about it, Satan is out to get us, and his attacks are more forceful than ever. The scriptures assure us that we can survive Satan's assaults by putting on the whole armor of God. In Ephesians 6:14 we read about the first essential part of that armor—the loincloth that really counts: "Stand therefore, having your loins girt about with truth." The same phrase is also found in Doctrine and Covenants 27:16. In these contexts *loins* refers to the life-giving power God has shared with us (or what we refer to in biology class as our reproductive organs—definitely vital areas to protect in any battle!). The word *girt* is the same as *gird*, meaning to surround or encircle. In preparing for battle with Satan, this admonition means to protect and defend our chastity and virtue. And with what do we protect them? With truth! Some might ask, "But how can truth protect us sexually?" Believe it or not, truth is our ultimate defense because, as President Boyd K. Packer has explained, "True doctrine, understood, changes attitudes and behavior."[1] Consider five prevalent myths associated with immorality and notice how the truth changes everything.

Myth 1: Friends, the Internet, and movies are my best sources for learning about sex.

The truth—parents and other trusted adults are your best source for sex education. I know you may think, *No way! I'm not talking about this stuff with my mom or dad!* Instead, you talk to friends, cousins, or older brothers and sisters. While it might seem easier to talk to kids closer to your age, the problem is that they rarely know what they are talking about. They pretend they do, and they want you to think they do, but don't settle for their inaccurate information. Whatever they think they know probably came from the Internet and movies, which usually present highly erroneous, unscientific, and exaggerated information about human sexuality. Such information is *not* sex education. It is actually sex mis-education marketed to make money. Producers of such material are not interested in your future happiness and well-being. They are only interested in their own financial gain. They couldn't care less that the images they are peddling are misleading and inaccurate—even dangerous.

Parents are the ones who have the knowledge, experience, and special interest in your welfare to guide you along. This is why a national survey that asked teens about the most influential voices in their sexual decisions found that young people rated parents significantly higher than their peers or the media.[2] You may feel awkward asking parents personal questions, and they may feel awkward answering them. They may even squirm a bit or clear their throats a lot. That's okay. Just be patient. Your parents really do want to talk to you about this stuff. They once went through exactly what you're going through and had most of the same questions you have. Give them a chance.

Some adults worry that by speaking frankly with young people about their bodies and sex they are somehow promoting or condoning promiscuous behavior. Assure them that the opposite is true. The most sexually active young people are usually the least informed. It is silence and ignorance, not open communication and truth that often lead to poor choices. In D&C 84:45 we read, "Whatsoever is truth is light." The more light we have, the easier it is to see and find our way. The more reliable information you gain from parents and other trusted adults, the more capable you are of making righteous and mature choices. All young people are curious about sex.

When that curiosity is met with real information from parents, young people are more willing to postpone sexual experimentation. In the national survey mentioned above, 88 percent of teens said talking with parents helped them delay sex. Parents and other trusted adults are your best source for information about sex. Armed with this truth, you will be better able to withstand Satan's attacks on your virtue.

Myth 2: Sexuality and spirituality are opposing forces.

The truth—sexuality and spirituality are supposed to be closely related. Some people have taught that the human body is evil and that sexual relations are worldly. Some religions consider people who do not marry and live lives of celibacy to be the most spiritual. The restoration of the fulness of the gospel dispelled the darkness and exposed these false perceptions and traditions.

In the context of the plan of redemption, we understand that receiving bodies is one of the primary reasons for which we came to earth. Our physical bodies, complete with sexual desires, do not pull us from God but give us the opportunity to become more like Him. Marriage between a man and a woman is not an alternative for those who can't live a higher law. It is the highest law. Latter-day Saints know that the greatest blessings that God can bestow await a man and a woman who are sealed for eternity. Sex within a strong and happy marriage is not just part of God's plan for us; it is right at the heart of it. As more people gain knowledge of this truth, Satan is furious because he is so envious of us. He will never have a body, a marriage, or a family.

President Spencer W. Kimball, in the April 1974 general conference, quoted Billy Graham's teaching that the Lord "'implanted the physical magnetism between the sexes for two reasons: for the propagation of the human race, and for the expression of that kind of love between man and wife that makes for true oneness.'"[3] In a healthy marriage, sex is a special expression of the unity, commitment, and love felt by a husband and wife. Moments of sexual closeness celebrate an emotional and spiritual bond that can draw a husband and wife closer to each other and closer to God. Elder Bruce C. Hafen and his wife Marie have written: "We restrain our passions and seek virtue not because romantic love is bad, but precisely because it is so good. It is not only good; it is pure, precious, even sacred and holy."[4]

A temple sealing is a sacred covenant and—though few may think of it like this—sexual relations between a husband and wife are a symbol of that covenant. Truman G. Madsen wrote, "The holiest of all achievements in this world . . . is to give your powers of creation and procreation mutually in the sacred relationship of marriage."[5]

To ask you not to think about sex or discuss it might be a

little unrealistic. However, I do not hesitate in the least to ask that it be discussed appropriately and respectfully. Joking about or making light of sex is as inappropriate and offensive as it would be to splash around in a baptismal font or have a food fight with the sacred emblems of the sacrament. Slang terms communicate irreverence for a sacred topic. It may take a little effort, but you can become comfortable calling body functions and parts by their proper names. You don't have to lower your language, attitude, or actions to the gutter or locker-room level when talking about a holy symbol of the covenant of marriage. Sexuality and spirituality are not meant to be opposites. Ideally, husbands and wives realize they can be interrelated. This truth provides the perspective that will help protect you from Satan's deceptions and counterfeits.

Myth 3: Commandments and standards are barriers keeping me from sexual satisfaction.

The truth—actually, the Lord's commandments and standards are instructions for success. That's hard to believe when you are at the doctor's office or grocery store and every magazine cover sports a headline like "10 Secrets to Great Sex." You feel like you are missing out because you have lived a sheltered life. You assume that everyone else must know secrets you don't because you are a member of the Church. Not so. Turn your thinking around. Church standards are not keeping you from anything. They are giving you something that others can only wish they had. I think I'll write an article for one of those magazines and title it "The Best-Kept Sex Secret in the World." Then everyone will open the magazine and read: "The Law of Chastity." The very rules you think are keeping you from what you want most are actually your ticket for obtaining it.

 Scan this QR code to watch a Mormon Message for Youth about the reasons why sexual standards are so important.

One research study reported that nine out of ten Americans have had premarital sex,[6] but that doesn't change the fact that those who delayed having sex until they were married enjoyed much greater sexual satisfaction and stronger relationships in their marriages.[7] In a global study that analyzed data from 59 countries, researchers reported that married couples reported having sex much more often than those engaging in sex outside of marriage.[8] These truths will help keep you strong in moments of temptation and pressure. Without this knowledge you might toss away your standards and disregard commandments, as many have done, but armed with these truths you can defend your choice to live virtuously.

Myth 4: Sex is something you get.

The truth—sex is most satisfying when it is given within the bonds of marriage. My blood type is A negative. The Red Cross loves me! They tell me only about 7% of people in the United States have that particular blood type, so I get called on often to donate. I've been happy to help through the years, but I have noticed that with the spread of HIV, hepatitis B and C, syphilis, and other infectious diseases, the donation process is more complicated than it used to be. Medical professionals have always checked my blood pressure, temperature, and pulse, but now they also ask point-blank lifestyle questions about everything from body piercing and tattoos to drug abuse to extramarital sexual experiences. Those who have indulged in such practices are often ineligible to give because it would be extremely dangerous for the Red Cross to use their blood. These people are rejected because their choices have made it so that, as much as they might like to help, they can't. They can receive, but they can't give. Each time I donate I feel thankful for the healthy choices I have made that allow me to give blood. The same is true when it comes to sex.

I once spoke to a young man who said, "I wish I weren't a Mormon for one day. I wish I had just one free day without all the rules and regulations."

"What would you do?" I asked.

"That's easy," he responded. "I'd smoke, I'd drink, and I'd have sex."

It was obvious that this young Latter-day Saint thought he was really missing out, but was he?

I asked if I could share an object lesson. When he agreed, I filled two cups halfway with water and explained to him, "One cup represents you. The other represents your friend. The water in both represents sexuality in your lives." Now, let me share with you the analogy I used for him.

Along comes someone who says pornography is no big deal. He says he doesn't know why the Church says it's wrong since everyone knows that it is just harmless adult entertainment. The person says pornography is just like looking at an art museum.

In response, you say, "I won't do that because I am a Mormon."

Your friend says, "Well, if it's just like looking at an art museum, what's the harm?" He becomes involved. He drinks from the cup and his level of water is lowered, while yours stays the same.

Then along comes someone who says masturbation is no big deal. He asks why the Church persists in saying it's wrong when all the health books say it's totally normal, that everyone does it, and that you shouldn't let anyone make you feel guilty.

In response you say, "I won't do that because I'm a Mormon."

Your friend says, "Well, if it's in the health books, why not?" He becomes involved. He takes drinks from the cup and lowers his water level even further, while yours stays the same.

Then along comes someone who says sex before marriage is normal and that as long as you love the person it's okay. He says as long as you're safe and protect yourself from disease and unwanted pregnancy then there is nothing wrong with it.

In response you say, "I won't do that because I'm a Mormon."

Your friend says, "Well, if you really love the person, why wait?" He becomes involved. He drinks from the cup, and before long the water is gone. His cup is empty while yours is not.

At first it may appear that he won and you lost, that he got something while you missed out. But let's fast-forward—not clear to the Second Coming or final judgment (as real as those times will be). Let's just fast-forward to your marriages.

You get married and your friend gets married. On the outside you look equivalent. You're both dressed up, enjoying a fun reception with family and friends. You both are posing for pictures in front of your wedding cakes. On the outside no one can tell you are different, but on the inside things are very different because your friend has nothing left to give. All he can do is take. Every sexual choice he has made since he was twelve—whether it was pornography, masturbation, or fornication—has taught his mind one thing and one thing only: complete and total selfishness. He shows up at his marriage ready to do what he has always done sexually—get, take. Anyone who is married will tell you how long that lasts. No one wants to be the one always giving to the one who is always taking. No one wants to be the constant faucet for the constant drain. Before long, things start falling apart. His selfishness starts to destroy his marriage and severely limits his sexual satisfaction.

Now let's compare him to you. Because you have chosen to live by LDS standards—the very rules and commandments that everyone laughs at or dismisses as old-fashioned—you still have water in your cup. You have not programmed your mind to always think of sex selfishly. If you have slipped up, you have repented. If you have fallen into a bad habit, you have had the courage to talk to your priesthood leader and seek the Lord's help in making positive changes. Because of this you still have water in your cup. You show up at your marriage with something to give as well as something to receive. On a firm foundation of trust and commitment (words you never hear in a locker room), love blooms. The more you give, the more you receive. The more you receive, the more you have to give, and soon you are caught up in a happy, healthy sexual cycle in your marriage that not only lasts, but gets better as time goes on.

"So," I asked the young man, "who really wins and who

really loses?" I hoped he was mature enough to recognize that, just as putting money in the bank takes self-discipline, living a morally clean life takes self-control. But those who put money in the bank have something to withdraw when others don't. In the same way, those who live the law of chastity are never left with an empty bank account. They have something to give.

According to the American Red Cross, someone in the United States needs blood every two seconds. In many cases these are life-and-death situations. Yet the percentage of eligible donors has shrunk to less than 38% of the population and that percentage gets smaller each year. Of course, some are disqualified for health reasons over which they have little control, but many are disqualified for lifestyle choices. They can all receive blood, but 62% of the US population can no longer give blood. Many have allowed their choices to limit their freedom and interrupt the natural give and take that keeps our lives balanced, whole, and satisfying.

Myth 5: I've already messed up. It's too late for me now.

The truth—because of the Atonement of Jesus Christ we can always start again. Not only can our sins be forgiven, but we can learn from our mistakes and our hearts can be changed. Sister Elaine S. Dalton has spoken often to young people around the world about the importance of guarding and protecting their virtue. In each group she addresses there are always heads that lower in guilt, depression, and despair. In such moments you can almost hear the lies Satan is telling these young people: "You've already blown it. There is no place for you in the Church now. You will always be a second-class citizen. No one will want to marry you. You are not good enough. You might as well give up." That's when Sister Dalton raises her voice and with great passion declares: "Because of [Christ] it is possible to be virtuous. And if one has not been virtuous, because of Him it is possible to return to virtue. . . . When we make a mistake, it is possible to repent because of His infinite Atonement."⁹

Perhaps as you have read this chapter you have felt twinges of guilt. Perhaps you have not always sought answers to questions about sex from appropriate sources or been respectful when talking about sexual things. Maybe you haven't always seen standards as being helpful and have made choices that have left you with a little less water in your cup than you wish. It is not too late. Don't turn away from the Savior and the Church thinking that will help ease your guilt. Turn toward the Lord and seek His grace, His divine power. His strength is perfect in our weakness (see 2 Corinthians 12:9). Not only is He willing to give us another chance to walk the strait and narrow way (see 3 Nephi 14:14; Matthew 7:14), but He is willing to walk with us (see Moses 6:34). The way is never so strait and narrow that there is not room enough for two—you and the Lord. You're not alone. He will not overlook sin, lustful desires, and selfish habits, but He will forgive sin, educate our desires, and help us through the process of replacing selfish habits with true charity—the pure love of Christ (see Moroni 7:47).

Satan's attacks are fierce and unrelenting. As his time is getting shorter he is throwing everything he can at us. He is not even trying to be subtle or sly. He knows exactly where we are the most vulnerable, and he is hitting, literally, below the belt. The only way to be protected is to put on the armor of God, to gird our loins with truth. As we choose to seek accurate sexual information from parents and other trusted adults instead of from the media, the light of truth will dispel the darkness. As we see sex as sacred rather than worldly and standards as steps to sexual fulfillment instead of barriers to it, we can make wise choices. As we live standards consistently, we are prepared to enter marriage ready to give as well as receive. And when we slip up we must never give up. Rather, we must look up! As we turn to the Lord, He will give us strength to repent and make positive changes. We will discover His love is perfect and His grace is sufficient (see D&C 18:31; Ether 12:26).

Armor Up!

Here are four ways you can gird your loins with truth. We invite you to take at least one (and hopefully all four) of these invitations.

1. Ask your parents or other trusted adults in your life for true information about sex rather than turning to friends, media, or other untrustworthy sources.

2. Treat the topic of sex in a way that respects its sacred nature. Don't joke around about sexual things with your friends, and avoid discussing them in a way that is overly casual.

3. Commit to follow all of the Lord's commandments with faith that you will be blessed for your righteous effort. Put the Lord's commandments to the test in your own life and prove to yourself that they will bring you blessings and happiness.

4. Always remember that your Heavenly Father and Jesus Christ love you. Don't hesitate to go to Them (and your priesthood leaders) for help if you are struggling. Remember that it is never too late to follow the Savior, and you have never messed up so much that He can't make it right.

Continue the Conversation . . .

What do being hungry, having to go to the bathroom, and getting a nose bleed have to do with keeping the law of chastity? Listen at seek.deseretbook.com/armorup as Brad Wilcox and the other authors share some of their own strategies for keeping the law of chastity in a world full of temptations.

 At seek.deseretbook.com/armorup, click on Roundtable Discussions to follow the authors' roundtable discussion for this chapter.

CHAPTER TWO

A BULLETPROOF BREASTPLATE

"Having on the breastplate of righteousness"
(Ephesians 6:14)

JOHN HILTON III

Which of the following do you think is the most important?

While they are all valuable, I think you'll agree that the heart is the most important. Did you know that your heart beats 100,000 times every twenty-four hours? During those twenty-four hours, the six quarts of blood inside you circulate "through the body three times every minute. In one day, the blood travels a total of 12,000 miles"[1]—that's like driving from Los Angeles to New York four times!

Let's face it, without a heart, we're not going to get much done. That's one reason why the breastplate of righteousness is so important—it covers and protects the heart. Though no one would choose to, we can survive without a hand, an ear, or an eye. But without a heart, the fight is over. That's why it needs special protection. Just as police officers wear bulletproof vests, we need a powerful breastplate to shield us from the attacks of the adversary. How can we put on the breastplate of righteousness? I suggest three ways:

(1) Get the word of God deep inside your heart,

(2) Live the standards, and

(3) Find your personal "commandments not a few."

Get the Word Deep Inside Your Heart

Sometimes we might think that our teenage years are a time for fun and experimentation and that we can focus on serious things like scripture study later. It's true that we should have fun in our teens, and there are some things (like different sports, school electives, or extracurricular activities) that we should try out to see if we like them. But it is also a time when we should be putting on the breastplate of righteousness by getting the word of God deep in our hearts. Speaking of the youth of the Church, President Henry B. Eyring said: "The pure gospel of Jesus Christ must go down into the hearts of students by the power of the Holy Ghost. It will not be enough for them to have had a spiritual witness of the truth and to want good things later. It will not be enough for them to hope for some future cleansing and strengthening. Our aim must be for them to become truly converted to the restored gospel of Jesus Christ while they are with us."[2]

Now is the time when the word of God should be carried into our hearts by the power of the Holy Ghost, and as a result our hearts should change. People in the Book of Mormon show us how to receive this mighty change. Let's look at some of their experiences. Enos said, "The words which I had often heard my father speak . . . sunk deep into my heart. And my soul hungered, and I kneeled down before my Maker, and I cried unto him in mighty prayer" (Enos 1:3–4). His father's words had gone into his heart, he felt a deep need, and so he humbled himself in mighty prayer. As a result, Enos became deeply converted to the gospel and declared it for the rest of his life (see Enos 1:26).

The people of King Benjamin heard the word of God that King Benjamin spoke and said, "Yea, we believe all the words which thou hast spoken unto us; and also, we know of their surety and truth, because of the Spirit of the Lord Omnipotent, which has wrought a mighty change in us, or in our hearts, that we have no more disposition to do evil, but to do good continually" (Mosiah 5:2). Because the word of God had gone into their hearts, their hearts were changed, and they didn't want to do evil any more. That is one of the blessings of putting on the breastplate of *righteousness*. If we lose the desire to break the commandments, it will be easier to be righteous. This change comes from planting God's words deep in our hearts.

Ammon taught King Lamoni and his servants the gospel of Jesus Christ. He read the scriptures to them and taught them God's plan. After King Lamoni had heard Ammon's words, he offered a mighty prayer and became converted to Christ. Later, Lamoni's servants testified "that their hearts had been changed; that they had no more desire to do evil" (Alma 19:33).

President Henry B. Eyring talked about those in the Book of Mormon who experienced this mighty change of heart. He said: "That mighty change is reported time after time in the Book of Mormon. The way it is wrought and what the person becomes is always the same. The words of God in pure doctrine go down deep into the heart by the power of the Holy Ghost. The person pleads with God in faith. The repentant heart is broken and the spirit contrite. Sacred covenants have been made. Then God keeps His covenant to grant a new heart and a new life, in His time."[3]

It's important to know that it can take time for the word of God to sink deep into our hearts and for us to experience this mighty change. It normally doesn't happen overnight. President Ezra Taft Benson taught, "For every Paul, for every

Enos, and for every King Lamoni, there are hundreds and thousands of people who find the process of repentance much more subtle, much more imperceptible. Day by day they move closer to the Lord."[4]

You can continue your journey towards a changed heart by seriously studying the scriptures, particularly the Book of Mormon. As you do so, the word of God will sink deep into your heart, you will feel less desire to do evil, and you will be excited to put on the breastplate of righteousness by keeping the commandments.

Live the Standards

Consider this analogy: A soldier is dropped off in enemy territory with specific instructions for how to get safely back to base once his mission is accomplished. Here is the map he is given:

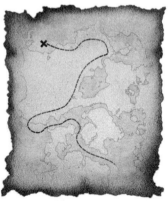

You can see from looking at this map that the directions don't give the most direct route back. If you were the soldier, would you try to go your own way? Sometimes people are tempted to do things their own way and ignore some commandments. Doing this is like taking off the breastplate of righteousness. Speaking of those who want to ignore the commandments and do their own thing, the Lord said, "They seek not the Lord to establish his righteousness, but every man walketh in his own way, and after the image of his own god, whose image is in the likeness of the world, and whose substance is that of an idol, which waxeth old and shall perish in Babylon, even Babylon the great, which shall fall" (D&C 1:16).

Hopefully, if you were given a map to safety you would follow it! The directions show you the safe route—just like the standards in *For the Strength of Youth* show us the safe route back to Heavenly Father. These standards are meant to make our lives better; they give us guidance we can follow. Why has God inspired prophets to give us those standards? Do you think that this booklet is just a practical joke that Church leaders play on teenagers to keep them from having fun? Absolutely not! Living the standards in *For the Strength of Youth* helps us put on the breastplate of righteousness.

Now here's something to think about—do you think it was fun for medieval knights to walk around wearing a breastplate?

My suspicion is that sometimes it was a little uncomfortable. But having an arrow go through your heart is even more uncomfortable. So while living the standards might not always be easy, *not* living the standards is much harder.

The Lord taught, "I give unto you a new commandment . . . Or, *in other words,* I give unto you directions" (D&C 82:8–9; emphasis added). The commandments are not meant to be annoying. They are directions that show us the right way, and they protect us, just like a breastplate.

Let's try a little experiment. Pick a number between 1 and 44. Any number. Now go get a copy of *For the Strength of Youth* and read what it says on the page number you picked. As you read, think about how living these standards could help protect your heart from spiritual damage.

I did this and picked page 11. Here's what I found:

> Satan uses media to deceive you by making what is wrong and evil look normal, humorous, or exciting. He tries to mislead you into thinking that breaking God's commandments is acceptable and has no negative consequences for you or others. Do not attend, view, or participate in anything that is vulgar, immoral, violent, or pornographic in any way. Do not participate in anything that presents immorality or violence as acceptable. Have the courage to walk out of a movie, change your music, or turn off a computer, television, or mobile device if what you see or hear drives away the Spirit.[5]

Think about the power of these words! There are so many suggestions for how to put on the breastplate of righteousness. Do we have any music that is "vulgar, immoral, violent, or pornographic *in any way?*" If so, let's delete it! Are we ever in a situation with friends where everyone is watching something inappropriate? Let's have the courage to be the one to stand up and leave.

Flipping a page or two further in the "Entertainment and Media" standard in *For the Strength of Youth*, we see additional ways we can put on the armor of righteousness:

> Take care that your use of media does not dull your sensitivity to the Spirit or interfere with your personal relationships with others. Spending long periods of time using the Internet or a mobile device, playing video games, or watching television or other media can keep you from valuable interactions with other people. Be careful that your use of social media does not replace spending time with your family and friends.
>
> Guard your safety and the safety of others by taking great care about what personal information and images you share through technology. Do not communicate anything over the Internet or through texting that would be inappropriate to share in person. Obey the laws that govern sharing music, movies, and other copyrighted items.[6]

Do we struggle with spending too much time in the virtual world? We can make a change! Do friends send us text messages containing things that we would be embarrassed to have our parents see? Let's have the courage to tell them to stop sending those messages! Are we tempted to illegally download media? Let's not justify it. Put on the breastplate of righteousness!

 Scan this QR code to watch a Mormon Message for Youth about how wise entertainment choices can help you put on the breastplate of righteousness.

All these examples come from just a couple of pages in *For the Strength of Youth*. As we carefully read this prophetic pamphlet, we will learn how to live the standards. Living these standards in righteousness will protect us from Satan's attacks.

Find Your Personal "Commandments Not a Few"

If you stop and think about it, breastplates probably aren't mass produced. Every person has a different size and shape and consequently needs a slightly different breastplate. When it comes to the "breastplate of righteousness," we all have different strengths and weaknesses, so each breastplate needs to be tailored to us personally.

In some ways, this can be a good analogy for the commandments. *For the Strength of Youth* gives important standards that everyone should follow. We know, for example, that every young man should prepare for a mission. We don't need any additional revelation to tell us that. God can also inspire each of us with additional personal guidelines that are tailored to bless us individually. In the scriptures this is referred to as "commandments not a few" (D&C 59:4). The Lord states that one of the blessings of keeping the commandments is to receive more commandments: "Yea, blessed are they whose feet stand upon the land of Zion, who have obeyed my gospel; for they shall receive for their reward the good things of the earth, and it shall bring forth in its strength. And they shall also be crowned with blessings from above, yea, and with *commandments not a few,* and with revelations in their time—they that are faithful and diligent before me" (D&C 59:3–4; emphasis added).

Commenting on these verses, Elder David A. Bednar said: "What are these 'commandments not a few,' and how do we receive them? . . . The individual and personal commandments 'not a few' we receive frequently tend to focus upon the good things we can and should do to develop and deepen our discipleship—as opposed to focusing primarily upon the bad things we must avoid or overcome. Such instructions typically are proactive and anticipatory in nature."[7]

"Commandments not a few" are personal guidelines that the

Lord gives to us. Find a peaceful time when you can prayerfully counsel with the Lord and ask Him if there are personal guidelines He would have you set for yourself. As you ask, your focus should be more on what more you might do to be a better disciple of Christ than on personal challenges or temptations that you want to overcome. These personal guidelines can bless you. The idea is that God can inspire us through the Holy Ghost to receive "commandments not a few"—guidelines that help us craft a breastplate of righteousness that protect us individually.

Put on the Breastplate

The principles that I've talked about in this chapter are related to each other. As God's word is planted in our hearts, we have less desire to do evil. At the same time, keeping the commandments makes it easier for the Holy Ghost to carry truth to our hearts. Elder David A. Bednar taught, "Only as [a person's] faith initiates action and opens the pathway to the heart can the Holy Ghost deliver a confirming witness."[8] As we are faithful in living the commandments we are blessed with additional "commandments not a few." Doing all of these things will help us put on the breastplate of righteousness.

We need this breastplate to be powerful because the heart is important! This vital organ of the body is protected by the breastplate of righteousness—likely the heaviest piece of the armor of God. But don't worry about the weight—you're strong enough to handle it. We can put on this breastplate by planting the word of God deep in our hearts, living the standards, and receiving "commandments not a few." As we do these things we will be strengthened against the "fiery darts of the adversary" (1 Nephi 15:24). Armor up!

Armor Up!

Here are three ways you can put on the breastplate of righteousness. We invite you to take at least one (and hopefully all three) of these invitations.

1. Help the word of God sink deep in your heart by beginning (or continuing) a habit of seriously studying the scriptures. Pray before reading each day and ask for the guidance of the Lord.

2. Choose one area in your life where you could more fully live the standards, and then make the changes you need to make. Consider this invitation from Elder Neil L. Andersen: "How do we decide where our repentance should be focused? . . . Humbly petition the Lord: 'Father, what wouldst Thou have me do?' The answers come. We feel the changes we need to make. The Lord tells us in our mind and in our heart."[9]

3. Pray and ask the Lord if there is a "commandment not a few" that He would like you to live by. Write down any impressions you receive and act on them.

Continue the Conversation . . .

You may think that "study your scriptures" is just a standard Mormon answer to everything and not take the advice very seriously. Come join the Knights of the Round Table at seek.deseretbook.com/armorup and hear some of their unique suggestions for bringing scripture study to life. Find out what John Hilton III says can be just as important to read as your scriptures.

At seek.deseretbook.com/armorup, click on Roundtable Discussions to follow the authors' roundtable discussion for this chapter.

CHAPTER THREE

PUT ON YOUR GOSPEL SHOES

"Stand therefore, . . . your feet shod with the preparation of the gospel of peace" (Ephesians 6:14–15)

ANTHONY SWEAT

Your feet need some love. I know, I know: It's all about the hair, the biceps, the clothes. (After all, when was the last time you heard a group of teenage girls talking about a boy and one of them said, "*Oh my heck*, he has the best looking feet I've ever seen!" That's what I thought.) But your feet should get some respect. Did you know that your feet have fifty-two bones in them, accounting for 25 percent of the bones in your entire body? The average person takes 10,000 steps every day, which adds up to about 115,000 miles over a lifetime (or four times around the planet). Your feet are the toughest part of your body, with the skin on the bottom of your feet being twenty times thicker than any other skin on your body. And when you run, your feet absorb pressure up to four times your body weight.[1] Let's give our feet some props.

When Paul gave his analogy of the armor of God, he told us to "stand therefore, having . . . your feet shod with the preparation of the gospel of peace" (Ephesians 6:14–15). Like our real feet, this part of the armor of God can sometimes be passed over quickly for more noticeable and flashy elements of the armor if we don't realize the importance this critical piece has in our spiritual success. The better we understand what it means for us to have our "feet shod with the preparation of the gospel," why it is so important, and how we can do it, the better we will be able to bless our lives and the lives of others with our sweet—and very important—feet.

"Feet Shod with the Gospel"

To have our "feet shod" literally means to put on some shoes and get ready to go.[2] In the context of the armor of God, having our "feet shod" means we need to be ready and put on our gospel shoes. That's right: gospel shoes (never knew those existed, did you?). Before you get too excited about getting these shoes, let me tell you a story to help. When I was a Primary kid, I was giddy to get baptized because our teacher had told us that when we got baptized we got to put on the armor of God. I thought that was a baptismal present: I was going to get the *actual* armor of God. "Are you kidding? We get real armor as a gift when we get baptized? Man, this church rocks!" They gave me a little card with my cut-out picture on it that I have saved to this day:

Putting on the
Armor of God!

Needless to say, reality came crashing down on me when I didn't see any squires or armor bearers ready to give me a sword at my baptism. So we're all clear, having our feet shod with the gospel of peace is a metaphor. (Don't be going over to your local shoe store asking if they have *Salvation Shoes* in a size 7.) "Feet shod" is a figure of speech that tells us that the best footwear for our mortal journey ahead is the gospel of Jesus Christ. We all know that different situations call for different shoes, and the wrong shoes for the wrong time can spell disaster: High heels on a basketball court? Air Jordans for snowboarding? Ski boots at a wedding? (Excluding marriages in Antarctica, of course.) Dress shoes while hiking? You get the point. To succeed at different events we must have the right footwear. And to spiritually succeed in mortality, we each must obtain and wear our own pair of gospel shoes.

When we have our feet shod with a preparation of the gospel it means we let the gospel of Jesus Christ direct our path in life (see Proverbs 3:5–6). It means that as we walk out of the door today, we base our actions and decisions and direction on the teachings of the Master. It means we "prepare the way of the Lord, and walk in his paths" (Alma 7:9). It means we avoid walking "in [our] own way, and after the image of [our] own god, whose image is in the likeness of the world" (D&C 1:16). Like a kid stepping in the giant snowy footprints of his or her father, to have our feet shod with the gospel means we head out the door ready to walk in Jesus' steps as He beckons us to "come follow me" (Luke 18:22).

Benefits of Gospel Shoes

Like all good shoes, the footwear of the gospel provides us with some great benefits (the best "soul" support on the market!). Three of the blessings we receive from wearing our gospel shoes and following Jesus' steps are these: *direction, protection,* and *projection.*

Direction: Your feet take you everywhere you will go in life. They will take you through high school and off to college. Your feet are going to walk you right toward a mission, marriage, and having a family (creating even more feet! Cute, little squishy ones at that!). Your feet will walk you into a career and Church callings. Eventually, your feet will walk you right through the door of mortality and into eternity. Ultimately, your feet will take you to stand in the presence of God to be judged of the paths you walked in life (see 1 Nephi 15:33). Think of all the places you will go, the situations you will find yourself in, and the things you will do in mortality! How exciting! And, potentially, how scary—scary because none of us, really, has any clue what tomorrow might bring and what direction life may take us. Proverbs 27:1 says, "Boast not thyself of to morrow; for thou knowest not what a day may bring forth."

However, the Lord knows. He promises us, "I know the end from the beginning; therefore my hand shall be over thee" (Abraham 2:8). This is the first reason why it is so important and critical for us to have our feet shod with the preparation of the gospel of peace: so we can receive direction from the Lord to choose the correct path in the myriad of situations we walk into throughout our lives. The Lord promises us that His gospel will "give light to them that sit in darkness and . . . guide our feet into the way of peace" (Luke 1:79). As we prepare ourselves with the gospel of peace, our gospel shoes will light the correct path our feet should walk. The scriptures teach us that the gospel is "a lamp unto [our] feet, and a light unto [our] path" (Psalm 119:105) that enables us to clearly see the direction we should take in life.

My wife, Cindy, and I have known each other since we were twelve years old. We went to the same junior high and high school, hung out with the same friends, and went to the same places. However, we never dated each other in school, and boy, am I glad. Not because she wasn't wonderful, but because neither of us was prepared with sufficient spiritual light to see the true eternal potential in one another. It wasn't that we were too young to see it; the problem was we were both too spiritually immature (me more so than her, of course). From age eighteen to twenty-one, both Cindy and I went away to different colleges (I also went on a mission during that time). We both went through immense spiritual growth and development during those years. When I came home from my mission and we began spending time together, we had both become spiritually prepared and mature enough to recognize that we were right for one another. Because of the light of the gospel, we could clearly discern that we should get married. Our spiritual preparedness—the gospel of peace—illuminated our path to walk to the altar of the temple. Had either of us not prepared ourselves with the gospel in the preceding years, we would have been either too afraid, too unprepared, or too blind to see the marriage path we should take. We would have had, spiritually, cold feet! The truth is that *our feet were only shod with wedding shoes because our feet were first shod with gospel shoes.* The light of the gospel showed us the path we should take, and it will give us each similar direction as we walk the path that Jesus shows.

Protection: Having your feet shod—or putting on shoes— also provides you with needed *protection.* As I was literally in the middle of writing this chapter, my eleven-year-old daughter Reagan let out a high-pitched, bloodcurdling squeal. When my wife and I ran into her room to see what was the matter, she was sitting on the floor holding her bare foot, with a one-inch-long needle sticking right through the bottom and out the side of her big toe. Man! That had to hurt. All of us who have ever had a sliver (or needle) in our foot can relate to what that feels like. The tiniest little foreign object can immobilize us and make it so we can only move forward gingerly. When we were kids, how many times did our parents shout to us as we were heading out to play in the summer, "Get some shoes on or you might step on a piece of glass or get a sliver"?

Similarly, our heavenly parents shout to us as we run out the door each day: "Get your gospel shoes on so you don't get cut by Satan!" Think of all the pins of pain and slivers of sin that the gospel of Jesus Christ protects us from! When we wear the protective shoes of the gospel we can avoid the scrape of selfishness, the frostbite of fornication, and the sliver of shame. Our lives can avoid the piercing thorns of guilt, despair, and anger if we will wear the shoes of the Savior. When we have our feet shod with the gospel of Jesus Christ, we put on spiritual combat boots that wrap and protect us against the shafts of Satan in the mortal war for our eternal souls (see Helaman 5:12).

Scan this QR code to watch a Mormon Message that gives some good insights into what can go wrong when we don't have the right shoes to protect us.

Projection: Not only does having our feet shod with the gospel protect us, but those gospel shoes *project* us onward and upward. Gospel shoes are *enabling* shoes. They are like a great pair of running shoes that cradle the foot, let the skin breathe, and support the sole. They are like basketball shoes that enable us to soar, hiking boots that give us the traction to climb mountains, and ice skates that help us glide swiftly. Similarly, the gospel of Jesus Christ enables us to run, soar, climb, glide, and do more with our lives than we could otherwise do on our own.[3]

I recently experienced this upward, enabling *projection* that comes from wearing gospel shoes as I finished my doctorate degree. The Lord blessed me, strengthened me, enlightened me, and enabled me to rise to the challenge of earning my PhD. During one critical statistics test, I worked on a problem for hours and couldn't calculate it right. I went to bed frustrated and prayed to God for help, saying something like, "Heavenly Father, I don't understand statistics, but *you* do! You know everything. Please, enlighten my mind through the Holy Ghost so I can understand these concepts." As I slept that night I had terrible dreams. All night long my mind was working through statistical calculations, analyzing Greek letters and solving for x. Talk about a nightmare! However, the next morning, just as I awoke I got a subtle little impression, "Go rework that stats problem you couldn't solve." Begrudgingly, I went to my desk, took a look at the problem, and immediately—miraculously—I could clearly see where I had gone wrong the night before. I knew exactly what do to. Within fifteen minutes I solved a problem that had stumped me for hours the night before. Some might dismiss that as luck or coincidence. Others might say I just was too tired the night before and needed rest. But I know that God enabled my mind through the night, clearing the mental blocks that were impeding my thinking, and gave me vision to work through and solve that problem. My gospel shoes *projected* me onward and upward in my schooling.

For the Strength of Youth teaches that as you strive to follow the gospel, "the Lord will make much more out of your life than you can by yourself. He will increase your opportunities, expand your vision, and strengthen you."[4] The footwear of the gospel of Jesus Christ will support, cradle, comfort, protect, and strengthen us to become our greatest selves as we run the marathon of mortality, enabling us to not only "endure to the end" (1 Nephi 22:31) and finish the race, but to run it in our best time possible. Now those are some sweet shoes.

Lacing Up our Gospel Shoes

Let's look at two ways we can lace up our gospel shoes:

First: *We must know the gospel.* Once while teaching a seminary class I gave the students a number of modern-day situations and asked them, "WWJD?—What Would Jesus Do?" Little did they know that the situations I gave them were based on actual stories from Jesus' life, and in many cases the students got the answer completely wrong, choosing the opposite of what Jesus had actually done. I told them, "It's tough to know WWJD when we don't know WJDD." (It's difficult to know what Jesus would do if we can't answer what Jesus *did* do.) This is our first lesson in how to prepare ourselves with the gospel of peace: we must learn and understand and act like the "Prince of Peace" (Isaiah 9:6). Of all the people on the earth who should know the gospel, it is those of us who have the restored gospel today! We have been given more pages of scripture, more prophetic teachings, and more access to gospel knowledge than perhaps any other people in the history of the world. We have no excuse, other than our own laziness, to not know the gospel. Let Jesus never say to one of us what He said to a Jewish leader named Nicodemus: "Art thou a master of Israel, and knowest not these things?" (John 3:10).

Thus, to have our feet shod with the preparation of the gospel of peace and let it direct our decisions, we must make a daily study of the gospel one of our primary goals in life. The gospel is so simple that a child can understand it, yet so comprehensive that we can study it for our entire life and barely scratch the surface of all it contains. Therefore, we must personally study our scriptures daily, attend and meaningfully participate in seminary and institute, consistently worship in our Sunday meetings, attend the temple as often as circumstances permit, and serve others. All of these things help us know the gospel so we can better follow its path. On a higher level, to really know the gospel we must practice it and have it become a part of us. Remember, *God Can't Be Googled!* The only way we can know the "things of God" is by the "Spirit of God" (1 Corinthians 2:11), and the only way we can have the Spirit of God is if we live the things we learn.

Second: *We must teach others.* Recently some have commented that we are having a "Mormon Moment"[5] in mainstream society. Puuuullleeeaaassse! The Mormon Moment will turn into a Mormon Minute, then into a Mormon Month, and eventually into a Mormon Millennium. This work will not be stopped. It will roll forward to the end of the earth, as prophesied (see D&C 65). But prophecies are only fulfilled as God's people are willing and able to fulfill them. A key to understanding how to have our feet shod with the gospel of peace comes from a verse in Isaiah where he also speaks of feet and peace: "How beautiful upon the mountains are the feet of him that bringeth good tidings, that publisheth peace; that bringeth good tidings of good, that publisheth salvation; that saith unto Zion, Thy God reigneth!" (Isaiah 52:7).

God needs more and more people who are capable of bringing good tidings of good, of publishing peace and salvation, and of explaining to and persuading others that God does indeed live and reign. This requires that we develop the capacity to clearly and articulately explain the gospel to others. God needs people who are not only faithful, but competent and confident in proclaiming the restored gospel. To this end, we must practice explaining the truths that we know to others. We must be able to give people short, easy, and accurate answers about basic gospel truths and standards. We must be able to talk about the Church with people of other faiths in a calm, confident, clear, and convincing manner. Think how you would answer some of the following questions that people really ask:

- What do Mormons believe about the Bible?
- Why don't you drink alcohol or coffee?
- Do Mormons think they will be the only ones who go to heaven?
- What do Mormons believe about being saved by grace?
- How do you know Joseph Smith was a true prophet?
- Why are traditional families so important in your Church?
- Why are you a Mormon?

When people ask these and other questions, you must "be ready always to give an answer to every man that asketh you a reason of the hope that is in you" (1 Peter 3:15). That is part of being prepared with our feet shod with the gospel of peace: publishing, proclaiming, and bringing gospel peace to others. As we do that our feet become sweet. As we do that we put on our gospel shoes and help others do the same. We can practice explaining the gospel at family home evenings and dinner discussions, in conversations with friends, at church and in seminary, and even in our minds or in the mirror!

God wants us to feel at peace, but He also wants us to publish peace to others. We must not only wear our gospel shoes for ourselves, but we must be able to tell others why we are wearing our gospel shoes and why they should buy a pair as well—for sale "without money and without price," of course (Isaiah 55:1). I add my testimony to that of Abinadi's that God blesses people who wear gospel shoes and who help others let the gospel guide their feet as well: "And again, how beautiful upon the mountains are the feet of those who shall hereafter publish peace, yea, from this time henceforth and forever!" (Mosiah 15:14–17).

Armor Up!

Here are two ways you can put on your gospel shoes and have your feet shod with the preparation of the gospel. We invite you to lace up your salvation shoes by acting on at least one of these invitations:

1. Think of a current decision you need to make or a problem for which you need direction. Study the scriptures and search for insights. Ask: What *did* Jesus do in a similar situation? What would He have me do in *my* situation? Seek for gospel truths that can illuminate the path you should take.

2. Go to Mormon.org and click on "FAQs" on the menu bar. Look up some of the questions people have asked you about Mormonism and learn how the Church answers similar questions. Practice giving a simple, clear, and confident answer to one of these questions to a parent or close friend.

Continue the Conversation . . .

Anthony Sweat says he loved his Air Jordan basketball shoes when he was growing up. In this roundtable discussion, Anthony and the other authors share how their gospel shoes have been even better. Find out what blessings of the gospel have been most meaningful to them at seek.deseretbook.com /armorup.

At seek.deseretbook.com/armorup, click on Roundtable Discussions to follow the authors' roundtable discussion for this chapter.

CHAPTER FOUR

SHIELDS UP!

"Above all, taking the shield of faith"
(Ephesians 6:16)

JOHN BYTHEWAY

Okay, true confession time. Here we go: When I was a kid, I watched *Star Trek*. No, that's not strong enough. I LOVED *Star Trek*. Do you even know the show I'm talking about? Maybe you've heard of the classic TV show, seen a re-re-re-run or two, or maybe you've seen one of the *Star Trek* movies. Anyway, my level of interest in *Star Trek* bordered on embarrassing, but I'm trying to make a point, and a man's gotta do what a man's gotta do, so it's all going to come out. I suspect you might have some questions. For example, you may be wondering . . .

Brother Bytheway,

Did you ever dress up in a *Star Trek* uniform? Yes. More than once. Halloween.

Did you ever own a *Star Trek* poster or calendar? Yes, but it was a gift.

Do you own any *Star Trek* movies? As a matter of fact, I own all of them.

Did you ever have a toy phaser or communicator? Yup. Both.

Did you ever attend a *Star Trek* convention? No. I promise.

I'm glad I could answer no on that last one, but I'm still as red as Captain Picard's uniform right now. Okay. It's out there. I feel better. Yes! I enjoyed watching the voyages of the starship *Enterprise*, under both Captain James T. Kirk and Captain Jean-Luc Picard.

Now, you may be wondering why I would share all this— I'll tell you. For just one reason—the word *shields*. Whenever the *Enterprise* would drop out of warp speed and enter an unknown planetary system, every Trekker watching the show knew that something interesting was about to happen. Sometimes I'd be sitting on the edge of the couch, and if the music suddenly became intense, I'd start yelling at the TV, "Shields! Shields!"

Sometimes the crew would raise the shields, but sometimes they waited too long and got hit by Klingon photon torpedoes or a Romulan disruptor. "Duh!" I would say to the TV as if the actors could hear, "Never enter any situation without your shields!"

Now, do you see why I shared my inner geek with you? Good. If it's still possible, we'll now make the switch from science fiction to spiritual fact. What I said on the couch as a tween is still true: "Duh. Never enter any situation without your shields."

The Shield of Faith

When Paul described the armor of God to the Ephesians, he said, in effect, "Shields up!" His exact words were, "Above all, taking the shield of faith, wherewith ye shall be able to quench all the fiery darts of the wicked" (Ephesians 6:16).

In the Apostle Paul's time, shields were *huge*. They weren't like the medieval shields we see in movies that are about the size of a large pizza or a garbage can lid. They were rectangular, about four feet tall and two feet wide, and they were often coated with a fire-quenching substance, since a flaming arrow was a weapon often used against them.

Soldiers would advance standing side by side, shields forward, forming a wide, walking wall. Since the soldiers held their shields out in front of them, their shields were the furthest thing from their body, ensuring that it would be the *first thing* to absorb any blows from the enemy.

Perhaps that's why Paul says, "*Above all*, taking the shield of faith." The shield was *above all*, being the first line of defense against their enemies and their weapons. With the exception of the sword, all of the other pieces of armor are also shields. A helmet is a shield for your head, a breastplate is a shield for your torso, shoes are shields for your feet, and so forth. But the shield of faith is the *first* shield, the shield "above all."

Shields and Faith

Faith, as you know, is the *first* principle of the gospel, which is another reason it is considered "above all." There are many kinds of faith—faith that things will work out, faith that the sun will come out tomorrow, faith that a sibling on a mission will be okay. The most powerful faith, of course, is "Faith in the Lord Jesus Christ" (Articles of Faith 1:4). The different types of faith we refer to in our gospel discussions all spring from and center in the most critical type of faith—our faith in Jesus Christ.

Like the Apostle Paul, Elder Vaughn J. Featherstone also used the words "above all" when he talked about the importance of having faith in Christ.

> Number one on our agenda, above all else, is faith in Christ. I don't know anything that will take the place of it. Whenever we find problems in the Church, we usually find them under one of two umbrellas or canopies, either transgression or lack of faith in Christ.[1]

In *Star Trek,* the shields were invisible, but teenagers equipped with the shield of faith are hard to miss. They walk differently, they talk differently, they see the world differently.

You can see it in their eyes, and you can see it in their step. They carry themselves with optimism and quiet confidence.

They go through many of the same problems other teenagers go through, but it's different for them. Why? They are *shielded*—shielded from despair and hopelessness because underneath it all, they have a sense that God lives, that He loves them, and that all things will work together for their good (see Romans 8:28; D&C 90:24). Satan's weapons bounce off their shields of faith.

Elder Marion D. Hanks explained it like this: "Faith, I believe, is to know that our Father will never quit caring; that He will never reject anybody; that He will never be satisfied until we, His children, have learned how to understand how much He cares."[2]

Teenagers with the shield of faith have made an important discovery: It's hard to have a negative attitude about things— in fact, it's hard to have a negative attitude about *anything*— when your life is built on Christ.

More Power to Shields!

So there I am, an eleven-year-old watching *Star Trek* after school. The starship *Enterprise* is under attack: projectiles rock the hull, the helmsman takes evasive action, and the captain gives the order, "More power to shields!"

On many days, your shield of faith works just great, and

you're like the teenagers described above. Other times, you may feel it weakening. Like on those days when life comes in and hits you, over and over, like a gang of angry Klingons in a Bird of Prey (a Klingon attack ship). That's when your shield of faith might begin to buckle, and you need more power.

When Paul chose to teach the Ephesians about how to survive spiritually, I don't think he was just searching for a random metaphor and somehow settled on the "armor of God." I think he chose armor on purpose. I believe he chose to talk about shields and swords and breastplates because he knew that life is a battle for each of us, and our faith is often challenged. In a recent broadcast, President Boyd K. Packer said that "you are growing up in enemy territory."[3] No kidding. And the enemy launches almost daily attacks.

And how are we attacked? With guns or swords or rocks? No. With "fiery darts." That sounds pleasant, doesn't it? The darts Paul was referring to were actually arrows. How would you like a million sharp, pointy things coming at you at high speed? Would you like it any more if the sharp, pointy things were on *fire?*! Flaming arrows can ruin your day (and leave annoying little soot spots on your clothes). Joking aside, what the scriptures call "the fiery darts of the adversary" (1 Nephi 15:24) are even more frightening.

Six Ways to Add More Power to Your Shields

Okay, back to the point (so to speak). How do we get more power to our shields of faith? There are a number of things we can do. As you know, there are places and activities that drain your faith, and there are places and activities that feed your faith. It's easy to tell the difference, and you know it. When we compromise on our standards, when we persist in looking at something we shouldn't, when we are unkind or rude or gossipy, we can literally feel the power drain on our faith. Suddenly, our confidence is not as strong, and we can feel our spirit crying out, "More power to shields!"

Well, the most obvious strategy for adding power to our shields is to do the things and go to the places that feed our faith. In the rest of this chapter, we'll talk about a few: Seminary, Scriptures, Seeing the Hand of the Lord, Sayings That Inspire, Sacrament, and Supplicate the Lord. (Wow. Did you notice they all start with *S*? How did that happen?) You may think you've heard all this before, but let's look at each one from a different angle.

Seminary Shielding. More than just the lessons, in seminary you surround yourself with other students who are also trying to strengthen their faith and raise their shields. You'll hear the testimony of your seminary teacher, you'll hear the testimonies of your classmates, and you'll even hear yourself share your testimony with others. Hearing others share their faith strengthens your own. Hearing yourself share your feelings strengthens *you*—as well as the people who hear you. Hearing and sharing the gospel adds power to your shields. Maybe that's why Paul wrote, "So then faith cometh by hearing, and hearing by the word of God" (Romans 10:17). There is a noticeable difference in the countenance of students leaving an inspiring seminary class compared to a group of students leaving, say, algebra or biology. Why would that be? The former have just added power to their shields.

Scripture Shielding. Scripture study is more than an item on a checklist. Read about those who have gone before, read about their struggles, and read how they grew their faith. They, like you, had times when they were under attack and their shields were weakening. Remember the man who said, "Lord, I believe; help thou mine unbelief"? (Mark 9:4). He was asking for more power.

Another thing: Have you ever added memory to your computer? I have. Many times. My computer is more powerful and runs faster when it has more memory. Similarly, the scriptures have an interesting impact on our minds. The stories of Jesus and Nephi and Paul become ours, because they actually add to our memories. Alma explained the impact of the scriptures to his son Helaman like this: "They have *enlarged the memory* of this people, yea, and convinced many of the error of their ways, and brought them to the knowledge of their God unto the salvation of their souls" (Alma 37:8; emphasis added). The experiences of the people in the scriptures are added to your memory, and this increases power to your shield of faith.

Watch this video and see how youth from Eastern Europe have put on the shield of faith by studying their scriptures.

Seeing the Hand of the Lord Shielding. It's not just about believing there is a God. It's about seeing His involvement in your life. Okay, another true confession: I'm not the best journal keeper. But I'm trying to improve. Usually, it has to be a big event for me to say, "Whoa, that's a journal entry." But that's the point. Record the big events in your life—or the small events that teach something big. Why? So that your children will *ooh* and *aah* at your experiences? Well, that's part of it, but not the best part. President Henry B. Eyring explained the best reason he found to write in his journal:

> Before I would write, I would ponder this question: "Have I seen the hand of God reaching out to touch us or our children or our family today?" As I kept at it, something began to happen. As I would cast my mind over the day, I would see evidence of what

God had done for one of us that I had not recognized in the busy moments of the day.[4]

When you take time to see the hand of the Lord in your life, to "count your blessings one by one," it might just "surprise you what the Lord has done."[5] You will realize that what you've heard at every youth conference you've ever attended is true—the Lord loves *you*. Yes, *you*. And He shows it every day if you look for it. And when you're having a bad day, or a bad week, you can pick up an old journal and remember how the Lord has helped you in the past, and be reassured that He will help you in the present. That will add power to your shield of faith.

Sayings That Inspire Shielding. I collect sayings and quotations, but it's about so much more than having a quote book to use in talks. When I was in college, I used to carry around a Franklin planner. It contained my calendar, an address book, and a bunch of other papers in a seven-ring binder. (Today, all of those things are in my smartphone.) People used to say to me, "Dude . . . you have a big planner," and I would always answer, "Dude . . . I have big plans." In my planner, I had a paper I called my "hope page." On my hope page were about a dozen sayings or sentences. Some were scriptures, some were lines from hymns, and some were phrases from my patriarchal blessing. If I ever needed "more power to shields," I'd turn to my hope page and read it. In less than one minute, I'd feel my faith growing.

May I recommend you do the same? Make yourself a hope page. Stick it in your scriptures, and make a copy for your smartphone if you have one. Look at all the things the Lord has said to you! Then you might put at the bottom of the page the same thing I did—a line from the hymn *How Firm a Foundation:* "What more can he say, then to you he hath said?"[6] Think about that. The Lord has said a lot of wonderful things to us. Our problem is, we forget. So remind yourself on a hope page so you can remember. Remind yourself of your own worth in the Savior's eyes. It will add more power to your shield of faith.

Sacrament Shielding. The sacrament isn't just part of the meeting—it's the reason for it! The Lord has arranged it so that we know exactly where we'll be each Sunday. Our worship service gives us a chance to repent and reflect on the past week of our lives. As we sing the sacrament hymn, and watch the priests break the bread, we prepare to hear the beautiful prayer in which we are promised that we can "always have his Spirit to be with [us]." The word *with* is a beautiful word. It means that you are never, ever alone. In the sacrament, the Savior promises to be *with you*, every day, all the time.

Elder Bruce C. Hafen visited the first international Especially for Youth (EFY) in Sweden. The youth were divided into smaller groups, and each group had chosen a special name for themselves. When Elder Hafen and his wife realized they hadn't chosen a name, they quickly settled on "With You." Elder Hafen explained to the youth:

> The Atonement simply means "with you," in two senses. First, it overcomes anything that separates us from our Heavenly Father, so we can be *with* Him; and Christ's Spirit can be with us—each day and forever. If we are faithful, some day, as He gathers us in, we will say, "O My Father, my Father, I am *with* you again."
>
> Second, only through the Atonement can we be with our family members and friends forever. . . . No longing is deeper than . . . our hunger to be with those we love. The Atonement forever fulfills those longings.[7]

When Jesus introduced the sacrament to the righteous Nephites and Lamanites, He promised, "if ye do always remember me ye shall have my Spirit to be *with you*" (3 Nephi 18:11; emphasis added). That's the beautiful promise of the sacrament, which provides a weekly infusion of power to your shield of faith.

Supplicate the Lord for Shielding. Supplication is more than just blessing those who are not here this week that they can come next week. Supplicating means really communicating with God. When I was sixteen years old, I remember one night reading the scriptures for seminary. This particular night still stands out in my memory, because I believe it was one of the first times I really felt the Spirit, and I knew it. The feeling came as I read some of the closing verses of Doctrine and Covenants 19, and they were about prayer:

> Pray always, and I will pour out my Spirit upon you, and great shall be your blessing—yea, even more than if you should obtain treasures of earth and corruptibleness to the extent thereof. Behold, canst thou read this without rejoicing and lifting up thy heart for gladness? (D&C 19:38–39).

Those verses hit me with power that night. I realized that I had just been given a formula for happiness that would be *better,* and more lasting, than if I had won the lottery and obtained the "treasures of earth." And after giving me the formula, it was as if the Lord was asking me in the next verse, "Can you even read this without rejoicing? Do you realize what I just shared?" I've never forgotten that night, or that verse of scripture. Reading it again always adds power to my faith. If you want to add power to your faith, then pray always. Pray when you feel like it, and pray even harder when you don't. Pray when you're happy, and pray when you're sad. He's your Father in Heaven, and He'll hear every word.

Time to Beam Out

I hope those ideas are helpful. It would be an even better idea for you to do some of your own pondering on this topic.

What are the things that build your faith? When have you felt your shield of faith weakening, and what have you discovered that increases its power?

In *Star Trek*, the crew explored "strange new worlds," going boldly "where no one had gone before." For us, we're not heading for a strange new world, we're going home. And it's not going to be strange; it's going to be *wonderful*. Paul taught, "Eye hath not seen, nor ear heard, neither have entered into the heart of man, the things which God hath prepared for them that love him" (1 Corinthians 2:9).

Life is not easy, but with the armor of God, we'll be okay. Each of us has our own battle between fear and faith, which rages every day. That's why we often hear the advice, "Keep the faith!" President Boyd K. Packer taught that you can feel a lot of emotions throughout your life, but be particularly careful to guard against fear:

> You can be worried and sad and disappointed, and all of the rest of it, but you are not privileged to be afraid. There is no fear in the work that we do. Fear is the opposite of faith, and if you have faith, you do not have fear. Those two things do not—cannot—exist simultaneously. So when you have a worry and a fear, you erase it with faith.[8]

I wish each of you the very best as you go forward in your lives. Strap on the armor of God, and forge ahead. With the

Lord's help, you'll quench all the fiery darts of the adversary and you'll accomplish wonderful things. And when you encounter any new situation, remember this little bit of advice from a former tween Trekker—"never enter any situation without your shields."

Armor Up!

Here are three ways you can use your shield of faith. We invite you to take at least one (and hopefully all three) of these invitations.

1. Make yourself a hope page. Stick it in your scriptures and make a copy for your smartphone if you have one. Look at all the things the Lord has said to you!

2. Think of three ways you can focus more on the Savior during the sacrament. Write the ideas down and try them out during sacrament meeting next week.

3. Think about your personal prayers. Are you really using your prayers as an opportunity for true supplication? Make a list of some areas in which you can improve your personal prayers, and focus on the items in that list one at a time.

Continue the Conversation . . .

Listen to this discussion with the Knights of the Round Table at seek.deseretbook.com/armorup and see how John

Bytheway and the other authors distinguish between having faith in a desired outcome and true faith in Jesus Christ.

 At seek.deseretbook.com/armorup, click on Roundtable Discussions to follow the authors' roundtable discussion for this chapter.

CHAPTER FIVE

BUCKLE ON YOUR HELMET

"And take the helmet of salvation"
(Ephesians 6:17)

HANK SMITH

Seventeen-year-old James woke up in a daze. Someone was calling his name.

"James, James, are you okay?"

James blinked, willing his eyes to focus. When his vision cleared, he could make out the press of teammates gathered around him, each one clad head to toe in football gear. Coach Sutherland leaned over him, his face tight with worry.

"Can you move?" he asked.

James felt weak and nauseated, but he managed a nod. "I'm all right," he said.

With Coach Sutherland's assistance, James found his feet and went in search of his helmet—the same helmet that flew off his head moments before he lost consciousness. He knew he had gotten lucky. Earlier that day, he had broken his helmet's chin strap and hadn't taken the time to fix it. More than once, his helmet had popped off, leaving him vulnerable to injury. He knew it could have been a lot worse and that next time he might not be so lucky.

Almost fifty years later, Elder James E. Faust of the Quorum of the Twelve Apostles (and later of the First Presidency) shared the lesson he learned that day playing football: "That was the only time that I was ever knocked unconscious. It was my own fault. I had learned a great lesson—it is always important to keep your chin strap fastened so that your helmet is in place and you have protection." He went on to compare his experience on the football field to wearing the armor of God: "Spiritual armor . . . protects against the many things that can knock us spiritually senseless."[1] As a young James Faust discovered, it pays to protect your head. You may not know it, but nestled inside your skull is a very valuable piece of equipment.

Your Amazing Brain

The three-pound mass of wrinkly tissue we call the brain has one million times the processing power of today's fastest computers. Your brain only accounts for about two percent of your body weight, but uses twenty percent of the energy you get from eating food. Think of it this way: Of the five pieces of pizza you ate last night, one of them went entirely to power your brain. This amazing machine continually receives signals from 130 million light receptors in your eyes, 24,000 hearing receptors in your ears, 10,000 taste buds, and hundreds of thousands of receptors in the skin, each with a specific mission to recognize touch, vibration, cold, heat, and pain.

Our brains have over 100 billion neurons—or nerve cells—that send chemical and electrical messages all day, every day, for our entire lives. They are like microscopic cell phones (with *much* faster service). Each one of these tiny cell phones in our brains can send 1,000 messages per second. (And you think *you* text a lot!) They relay messages back and forth that enable us to blink, walk, talk, chew, run, dream, text, and everything else we do during the day. Right now, your brain is sending millions of messages throughout your body that control how you hold this book, how you breathe, how you read these words.

All of our emotions come from our brains too. How does it feel to love another person? Have you ever had a crush on someone? The heart is the symbol for love, but the feeling of love actually comes from the brain. Without it, we wouldn't know the joy of love. (Imagine on your wedding day turning to your new eternal companion and saying, "I love you with all of my brain.")

Our brains are also incredible recording devices. We've all seen something, heard something, smelled something, or tasted something that evoked powerful memories and emotions. I love to listen to music when I run. Whenever I hear a song, it always amazes me that I can remember exactly where I was running the last time I heard it. Everything that comes through our eyes, ears, nose, and mouth is logged in our brains. The more often we experience something, the more clearly it is recorded and available for recall. As an exercise, I want you to do each of the following in your mind:

- Picture a map of the country in which you live.
- Picture the faces of your best friends.
- Picture your parents laughing. Now, picture them angry. Now, worried. Now sad.
- Picture the face of the prophet.
- Picture the temple closest to your house.

No computer in the world could possibly do what you just did in the time you did it. Your mind has recorded your whole life and is now stocked full of knowledge, experiences, feelings, and memories. No wonder President Gordon B. Hinckley said: "I marvel at the miracle of the human mind. . . . No computer or other creation of science can equal the human brain. What a remarkable thing you are. You can think by day and dream by night. You can speak and hear and smell. Look at your finger. The most skillful attempt to reproduce it mechanically has resulted in only a crude approximation. The next time you use your finger, watch it, look at it, and sense the wonder of it."[2] Have you ever thought of your fingers as marvelous creations? Go on, take a look. All of the components—your joints, your ligaments, your bones, your flesh, your muscles—must all work together in order to function properly. And in control of it all is your wonderful, marvelous brain.

Besides keeping us alive and enabling us to walk, talk, and move, our minds are our spiritual centers. Our brains process our feelings, preserve our memories, and, in turn, use this information to shape our identity—temporal as well as spiritual. Like a computer picking up on wireless Internet, our brains are the connection to our Heavenly Father's messages to us. Having a healthy and clear mind is vital to gaining and maintaining our testimonies and receiving divine direction. Our brains are the key to answering life's most difficult questions and making life's most difficult choices. We only get one brain during our lives, so we'd better take care of it. We want our minds to be pure so we can have crystal-clear reception for communication with our Heavenly Father.

Protect It!

Now that you understand how important your brain is to both your physical and spiritual life, it is up to you to protect and guard it from any harm. Everyone knows it is smart to wear your helmet when you are riding a bicycle, a skateboard, a motorcycle, or when playing contact sports. Even skydivers wear helmets. (I don't know how this helps, but way to play it safe, skydivers!) Why do most of us take the time to put on a helmet? Because we like being alive and we like our brains to stay inside of our skulls. Brain inside skull—good; brain outside skull—not so good.

When I was younger, I hated the way my bicycle helmet looked on me. I thought it made me look weird. (Now that I'm older, I can see that I looked that way whether I had the helmet on or not.) If looking weird in a helmet is a worry for you, please remember something that my dad said to me when I complained: "You'll look a lot weirder when you're picking pieces of pavement out of your head." When he put it that way, I was much less hesitant to strap the helmet on. Sure, a hoodie or a baseball cap probably would have looked more fashionable, but I only had one brain and I needed to protect it.

Besides protecting our mind from anything that could smash it (the road, a car, your sister's fist), we must also guard it from things that damage it without causing head trauma. Once the brain absorbs images and other sensory information, it's nearly impossible to get any of it back out. Having everything you see, hear, smell, and taste recorded in your brain is both a wonderful blessing and a horrible curse. I love to remember the fun times I've spent with my family or laughing with friends, but I literally feel sick when I remember the times when I've made selfish choices and hurt others. We all have peaceful confidence and complete heartache when we are alone with our memories.

Can you see why we must vigilantly guard what is allowed to enter our minds? One of the reasons that drugs and alcohol are evil is because they can permanently damage the mind. President Gordon B. Hinckley said, "The drug-induced damage to self-worth and self-confidence is almost impossible to restore."[3] Look for all of the ways drugs affect your mind in the following quote from *For the Strength of Youth:*

> Avoid any drink, drug, chemical, or dangerous practice that is used to produce a "high" or other artificial effect that may harm your body or mind. Some of these include marijuana, hard drugs, prescription or over-the-counter medications that are abused, and household chemicals. Use of these substances can lead to addiction and can destroy your mind and your body. Addictions harm your physical, mental, emotional, and spiritual well-being. They damage relationships with family and friends and diminish your feelings of self-worth. They limit your ability to make choices for yourself. If you are struggling with any type of addiction, seek help from your parents and your bishop now.[4]

Like drugs, pornography is evil because it can cause permanent damage to the mind. Elder Dallin H. Oaks said: "A person who feasts upon filthy stories, or pornographic or erotic pictures and literature, records them in this marvelous retrieval system we call a brain. The brain won't forget this filth. Once recorded, it will always remain subject to recall, flashing its perverted images across your mind and drawing you away from the wholesome things in life."[5] Pornography is a drug. It causes the brain to become addicted to its own chemicals. The addiction forces the brain to produce those chemicals more and more until they are being created in amounts that actually damage the brain that is creating them. This slow drowning sinks the addict deeper and deeper into the addiction. Carefully read this uncompromising warning in *For the Strength of Youth*:

> Avoid pornography at all costs. It is a poison that weakens your self-control, destroys your feelings of self-worth, and changes the way you see others. It causes you to lose the guidance of the Spirit and can damage your ability to have a normal relationship with others, especially your future spouse. It limits your ability to feel true love. If you encounter pornography, turn away from it immediately.[6]

It is easy to see why Nephi's brother Jacob wrote that we have "delicate minds" (Jacob 2:9). Delicate things can be dented or broken easily. At night, when you gaze up at the moon and all its craters, keep this quote from Elder Jeffrey R. Holland in mind: "Tragically, the same computer and Internet service that allows me to do my family history and prepare those names for temple work could, without filters and controls, allow my children or grandchildren access to a global cesspool of perceptions that could blast a crater in their brains forever."[7]

Putting on the helmet of salvation can help you make good choices with what you do online. Watch this video and learn why it's important to "watch your step."

The helmet of salvation that Paul lists as part of the armor of God (Ephesians 6:17) can protect you from being knocked spiritually senseless with a crater in your brain. The word *salvation* means deliverance from harm or ruin. The standards in *For the Strength of Youth* make up the helmet that can completely protect your mind from irreversible harm and complete ruin. The helmet of salvation is impervious to all of Satan's pounding. When we have the helmet of salvation tightly secured, our minds, our memories, our relationships, our identity, and our spirituality are all safely protected.

We buckle on the helmet of salvation when we choose to offer personal and sincere prayers to our Heavenly Father. We strap on the helmet when we choose to search our scriptures for truths that we can live by. We buckle on the helmet when we attend church, when we go to seminary, when we choose good friends, and when we go to the temple. When we make mistakes, we put our helmets back on by repenting and making positive changes. We buckle on the helmet every time we choose the Lord's way over any other way that is offered to us.

Some may be concerned that wearing the helmet of salvation will make them look about as cool as I looked in my bike helmet. Don't allow the fear of what others may think about you control your choices. The standards you have chosen for yourself might not allow you to fit in with some groups, but you will please those who matter most—the Savior and yourself. The helmet's purpose is not to make you look good; its purpose is to protect you and your future by not allowing drugs or pornography to contaminate your mind. It protects your ability to communicate clearly with your Heavenly Father.

When my wife, Sara, was a junior in high school she had a crush on a senior in one of her classes. She was hoping with all of her heart (or *brain*) that he would ask her out on a date. (No, it wasn't me. Can you believe it?) Her wish finally came true and one day he asked her to go to a movie on a triple date with some of his friends. As the day for the date approached, she was getting more and more excited.

He picked her up the night of their date with a car full of other seniors. As they pulled out of her driveway, she asked her date what movie they were going to see. When he told her the name of the movie, her heart sank because she knew it didn't fit the standards she had chosen to live by. What was she going to do now? She was nervous to say anything because she was the youngest person in the car and all of these kids had been friends with each other for a long time. After a few moments, she leaned over to her date and said, "I don't think I can see that movie." She was nervous and apparently said it too quietly because he turned the radio off and said, "What was that?"

In the sudden silence, everyone in the car was listening, and she went from nervous to terrified in a single moment. However, Sara had self-confidence because she lived her standards. She took a few seconds to think about what to say. Her confidence quickly returned and she said, "I'm sorry, I really don't want to see that movie."

The silence in the car seemed to go on forever until one of the boys in the back of the car said, "Well, what do *you* want to do?"

Again, silence. At that moment she remembered that her date had once told her how much he liked indoor soccer. (Remember what I said earlier? Like a computer picking up on wireless Internet, our minds are our connection to our Heavenly Father's messages to us.) She said, "Why don't we go play indoor soccer?"

Her date smiled and said, "That's a great idea."

The six of them spent the evening in the church gym

playing soccer and they ended up having a great time. (Luckily, a much more handsome prince entered her life a few years later.)

Sara's story is an example of how the helmet of salvation protected her mind. She had decided a long time before that night what she would allow herself to see and hear. No matter the consequence, she decided to keep that helmet on. Decisions like this protected her future and have made her the incredible person she is today.

Buckle On That Helmet

Nobody wants to get knocked spiritually senseless. President Faust was able to recover from his poor decision at a football practice, but we might not be so lucky. The Lord has given us an amazing mind capable of feeling great love for others and receiving personal revelation, and He expects us to protect it by putting on the helmet of salvation. Don't take the risks Satan wants you to take. Without your helmet, you and your future are exposed to the heavy sledgehammer of sin. If you leave your helmet on the sidelines, your ability to love others and your ability to communicate with your Heavenly Father may be reduced to rubble.

As we buckle on the helmet of salvation, we will be able to walk through the deceptions all around us without being harmed. Our self-confidence will increase. We will be virtuous and happy in a world continually bombarded and damaged with sin. We may make some mistakes, but we can put our helmets back on. No matter the decisions of the past, it is not too late for you. Pick up your helmet, buckle it on, and press forward with confidence. As we navigate our way through sin, one day we will look up and discover that we are safely home, back in the arms of our Heavenly Father and our Savior.

Armor Up!

Decide that you are never going into another day's battle unprotected. You can start right now. Here are three things you can do to put on the helmet of salvation. We invite you to take at least one (and hopefully all three) of these invitations:

1. Talk with your family about the type of media in your home. What can you do as a family to make sure harmful things won't come into your home through television, phones, or the computer?

2. If you have not already done so, make a firm and prayerful decision to completely abstain from drugs, alcohol, or anything else that could damage your mind.

3. Get rid of any pictures (on your walls, in your locker, CD covers, DVD covers, and so on) that don't fit with the standards outlined in *For the Strength of Youth,* and replace them with pictures that do.

Continue the Conversation . . .

Media is a topic that can easily divide people. Even within the Church everyone seems to have different opinions and ideas about what is "good" and exactly where the line should be drawn. Find out how Hank Smith and the other authors determine what media to include in their own lives. Their ideas at seek.deseretbook.com/armorup may help you.

At seek.deseretbook.com/armorup, click on Roundtable Discussions to follow the authors' roundtable discussion for this chapter.

CHAPTER SIX

YOUR SPIRITUAL SWORD

"And take . . . the sword of the Spirit, which is the word of God" (Ephesians 6:18)

LAUREL CHRISTENSEN

I had the chance to teach some younger children in Primary. They found out that "Sister C" (so much easier to say than "Sister Christensen") didn't have a husband yet and then figured out that meant I lived alone. And that really bothered them. It bothered them enough that they brought it up several times, and I just couldn't figure out how to help them feel okay about the fact that I lived alone.

One Sunday the lesson was on the Holy Ghost, and it dawned on me that this was the perfect opportunity to ease their concerns.

"Now, I know you have been worried about me living alone. But I don't actually live alone—I have a roommate!" They seemed interested.

"My roommate is the Holy Ghost. He is always with me."

The children seemed satisfied as we talked about what it means to have the companionship of the Holy Ghost. But I learned what a bad communicator I must be when I found out later in the week that one of the children had asked his parents if he could visit "Sister C."

When asked why, the answer was simple: "Well, the Holy Ghost lives with her and I'd like to meet Him."

I love that little story, but even more, I love the truth that I came to learn because of it.

And the truth is, I *do* have the Holy Ghost living with me . . . or at least I can.

I have had many times when I have felt a desperate need for the companionship—the literal companionship—of the Holy Ghost. Here are some of those times:

- When my garage got broken into after moving to a new home and I had to sleep for several nights with my lights on.
- When my youngest brother was sealed in the temple and I was feeling a sense of dread at going alone and being the last one in the family still single.
- When I have had to make any big decision on my own and there really hasn't been someone who could help me figure it out except Heavenly Father.

But you don't have to be single to see the importance of

the constant companionship of the Holy Ghost (and yes . . . I said *constant*).

Quick—think:

When was the last time you know you felt the companionship of the Spirit? If it wasn't some time today, you are missing out *and* you are missing a really important piece of armor: "The sword of the Spirit, which is the word of the Lord" (Ephesians 6:17).

How can the constant companionship of the Holy Ghost be a part of our armor?

One of my favorite hymns is "Let the Holy Spirit Guide":

> *Let the Holy Spirit guide,*
> *Let Him teach us what is true.*
> *He will testify of Christ,*
> *Light our minds with heaven's view.*
>
> *Let the Holy Spirit guard,*
> *Let his whisper govern choice.*
> *He will lead us safely home*
> *If we listen to his voice.*
>
> *Let the Spirit heal our hearts*
> *Through his quiet gentle power.*
> *May we purify our lives*
> *To receive Him hour by hour.*[1]

The Holy Ghost is our sword as He *guides* us in truth, as He *guards* us in our choices, and as He *heals* our hearts. Before we talk about how the Spirit is your sword, you need to understand why the Holy Ghost is so important and how you know when you are enjoying His companionship.

When Christ was getting ready to leave the Nephites after His visit to the Americas, His disciples knelt in prayer, "and they did pray for that which they most desired" (3 Nephi 19:9).

Think for a minute. What is the thing you might *most desire* if you could ask your Father in Heaven for anything? Here were the disciples in the presence of Jesus. They could have asked for Him to stay. They could have asked that nothing bad would ever happen to them again. They could have asked that they'd be given everything they needed to live a comfortable life.

But they didn't.

Instead they asked for the thing they "most desired." And that desire was "that the Holy Ghost should be given unto them."

Wow! Did you read that?

Of *all* the things they could have asked for, they asked for the companionship of the Holy Ghost. *Why?*

Well, one of the answers can be found earlier in the Book

of Mormon. "The Holy Ghost will show unto you *all* things what ye should do" (2 Nephi 32:5; emphasis added).

All things? Really? Yes. Really.

And that is why the Spirit can *guide* and *guard* and *heal*—because He can show us all things we need. So, if you had the chance to ask for the one thing that would help you know and see everything you needed to, that would help guide you and guard you from danger and heal your heart so you could have the happiest life you could, is there really anything else you would want to ask for?

I can't imagine there would be.

I believe that there are a lot of people walking around with little plastic knives of the Spirit instead of the mighty sword of the Spirit. And I think one of the reasons is that they don't know they have access to the sword of the Spirit—they actually aren't entirely sure what the Spirit feels like or how the Spirit speaks to them.

And *what* the Spirit can do for you only matters if you know the *how* . . . for *you*.

Learning How the Spirit Speaks to You

We learn how the Spirit feels from the New Testament:

"But the fruit of the Spirit is love, joy, peace, longsuffering, gentleness, goodness, faith, meekness, temperance" (Galatians 5:22–23).

So, according to Paul (who is writing to the Galatians here), if you are feeling *love* or *joy* or *peace* or *patience*, if you are feeling *kind* or like you want to do something *good*, you are feeling that way because of the Spirit. Does that mean any time you are feeling those feelings, you are feeling the Spirit? Yes. I believe it does.

Too often we think we have to be at a youth conference testimony meeting where everyone is crying or we have to be dressed for church to feel the Spirit. But the truth is, we should be able to feel (and recognize—that's the important part) the Spirit every single day in a variety of settings—at the breakfast table with our family, walking in the halls at school with friends, after school when we don't get frustrated with a younger brother or sister, at night when we say "good night" to Mom and Dad. Remember, you are promised through the sacrament that you can "always have his Spirit to be with [you]" (Moroni 4:3). Always! So, you should be experiencing the "fruits of the Spirit" or the feelings of the Spirit every day— many times a day!

And that is the beginning of understanding *how* the Spirit communicates to us.

I think it's tempting to want an owner's manual to understand how the Spirit speaks to you. But I've learned over my life that a manual can't be written for you by anyone *but* you. It's perhaps one of the most personal things we must come to know for ourselves. Someone told me once that learning to know how the Spirit communicates to you is like learning a foreign language. And the one who knows the language is the only one who can teach you.

Yes. That's exactly what I mean. The Spirit Himself has to teach you how He teaches you. And unless you find out *how* the Spirit communicates with you, you can't completely suit up and add the sword of the Spirit to your armor.

And why is the sword important? Well, because all the other pieces of armor are protection from whatever the adversary throws at you. But, the sword allows you to actually *do* something when you are being attacked. It's the only part of the armor that lets you play defense *and* offense. Having a weapon is pretty important when arming yourself for battle, don't you think?

The Spirit is *your* secret weapon when fighting against the evil and temptations and challenges of this life. Brigham Young taught that "we live beneath our privileges" in terms of receiving revelation from God for guidance.[2] You might be tempted to think this is because the Spirit isn't communicating with you or that you aren't worthy to receive communication from Him. But I believe, more often than not, we are living beneath our privileges because we don't recognize how often we are receiving that important communication.

And so you have to know how the Spirit is communicating

to you in order to use Him as your weapon. But learning this takes some time and effort.

Elder Neal A. Maxwell taught that "revelation is not a matter of pushing buttons but of *pushing ourselves*, often aided by fasting and by scripture study."[3] You've likely had the experience of pushing yourself to do something hard at school or in sports. But have you pushed yourself to find out *how* the Lord tries to talk to you or tries to help you through the Spirit?

I have.

And it started for me when I was in kind of a desperate situation to receive some personal revelation. I was reading some verses in the Doctrine and Covenants that I had gone to many times before when I was looking for an answer:

"Behold, you have not understood; you have supposed that I would give it unto you, when you took no thought save it was to ask me. But, behold, I say unto you, that you must study it out in your mind; then you must ask me if it be right, and if it be right I will cause that your bosom shall burn within you; therefore, you shall feel that it is right" (D&C 9:7–8).

It was like a light went on inside me and I realized that this wasn't about me finding the answer I was looking for—this was about me finding out *how* the Lord was trying to give me my answer.

And so I set out that day on a little quest to learn how it

is the Spirit speaks to me. I went to my Father in Heaven in prayer and I would say things like this:

"I'm feeling . . ."

"And when I feel this way, I think the Spirit is trying to tell me . . ."

"Is this right? Is this how the Spirit speaks to me?"

This wasn't a process that happened in a day. In fact, it didn't even happen over several days. But, over time, I started to learn exactly how the Lord used the Spirit to speak to *me*—not to my friends, not to my parents, not to the prophet, but to *me*.

And it's something you have to learn for yourself if you want to arm yourself with the sword of the Spirit.

Are you ready to find out? To really find out how the Spirit communicates with you? Here are some steps to help you pick up and use your sword:

Start Living as If the Spirit Is Speaking to You

Joseph Smith taught: "No man can receive the Holy Ghost without receiving revelations. The Holy Ghost is a revelator."[4]

So, do you have the gift of the Holy Ghost? Then you are receiving revelations. So tomorrow morning, I want you to wake up and live like the Spirit is speaking to you: All. Day. Long.

You see, I woke up one morning and made a conscious

decision to believe that if I was worthy (not the same as perfect!), God, through the Spirit, was communicating with me. I chose to live as if He were talking to me, whether I recognized it or not.

The Book of Mormon teaches that "everything which inviteth or enticeth to do good" is from God (Moroni 7:13). So I chose not to hesitate. If I had an impression to do something good, I acted. And when I did, I could almost always see that it was an impression from the Spirit.

A young woman asked me once, "How do you hear the Spirit so much?"

My answer was simple (and still is): "I don't wait anymore, wondering if it's the Spirit or not. If it's an impression to do something good, I just assume it's the Spirit and I act on it." I'm showing the Lord how I think He communicates with me and trusting that He'll help me learn.

Something will happen when you choose to live as if God is talking to you through the Spirit. You will very soon discover that He *is*.

Watch a video about a young man who acted when the Spirit spoke to him. The results are pretty incredible.

Give Him Opportunities

There are so many different places the Spirit can speak to us.

When I was a missionary, we taught a man named Bill. Bill was a brick mason from Kentucky, and before his baptism, someone he worked with saw Bill standing still on the roof of the building he was working on. This man asked Bill what he was doing. Bill's response was simple: "I'm pondering." Bill learned early on in our discussions that that was how the Spirit spoke to him. When he made time to just be still and think, Bill received revelation.

Some people feel like they can most easily hear the Spirit at the temple. Others experience clearer communication when praying or fasting or reading the scriptures.

The point is we are all different and the easiest place for me to get revelation might not be the same for you. But you have to know what method the Spirit most often uses to communicate with you. What if the very way He uses involves an activity where we spend the least amount of time?

I've learned that all those places—moments of being still and pondering, going to the temple, kneeling in prayer, participating in fasting—can work for me. But nothing seems to help me hear or receive revelation more clearly than when I am immersed in my scriptures. I've been amazed at how many times I've received a direct answer from the printed pages of God's word.

So . . . what if I don't make time for scripture study?

I could read you pages and pages from my journal about times when I've been struggling and I've been doing all of those good things (pondering, going to the temple, praying, and so on) and I am certain the Spirit was communicating to me. But then I open my scriptures and the answer seems to jump right out at me.

If you do not know the best method for you to hear the voice of the Lord in your life, you need to commit to spend time with all of them until you find the one that seems to be your best fit.

All of those things work, and we might be blessed that any one of them works perfectly fine for us. But, just as we all learn things at school through different methods, we might learn through the Spirit differently, and our Father in Heaven knows the best way to reach us. We need to be sure we are giving Him every opportunity.

Spend time quietly pondering. Make time for the temple. Stay on your knees a little longer. Have a meaningful fast. Read your scriptures every day. Provide opportunities for the Spirit to speak to you, and you will be amazed to find out how clearly He does.

Remove Interference

I used to coordinate large public events for a living and relied heavily on my smartphone to get my job done and to communicate with my team. At one event, my phone froze. It had happened before and I knew that I just needed to take my battery out and count to ten. So that's exactly what I did this time.

But nothing happened. A blank screen showed up with an error message that read: "Incompatible or corrupt system."

It didn't seem to matter how many times I took the battery out or even how many times I said a little prayer and asked the Lord to help me. I would take the battery out, count to ten (or one hundred), put the battery back in, and . . . nothing.

The entire event was much more difficult without my phone. I was so frustrated and a little discouraged that heaven hadn't helped fix my phone.

When I got back to my hotel room that night, I was pretty discouraged. Ninety minutes on a tech support line produced nothing. But when I told the guy about the error message, he said, "The only thing that would produce that kind of message would be a third-party application."

"What?"

"A third-party application. Something that wasn't on the

phone when you got it. You would have had to install it on your own."

I had a little "ah-ha" moment with my smartphone. Shortly after getting it, I had chosen to install a popular app (i.e., a "third-party application"). Before it installed, I read some warning about it not being officially authorized . . . might cause problems . . . they weren't liable . . . I even remembered seeing a warning from a friend of mine online that this particular app had crashed his phone. But surely I was different, right? So I installed it and a few weeks later, the phone crashed.

I synced it up again.

I put the app on *again*.

A few days later, the phone crashed.

I synced it up again.

I put the app on *again* . . . and twenty-four hours later, it crashed . . . again . . . at the event I was working.

And the Spirit taught me something really important. Sometimes we allow "third-party applications" into our life— things that aren't compatible with our spiritual operating system to begin with. We choose to let these sins in, or "install" them. Sometimes they even come with a warning of sorts. And we might get warnings from others. But we think it doesn't apply to us. Surely we are different. Surely we will be okay.

But, here's the thing. *Any* "third-party application" we

install that isn't manufactured by heaven will create interference in our ability to communicate with our Father in Heaven. And sometimes, once we've let it in, even though He *can* fix everything and make it right, He won't. There are natural consequences to our choices and when there is a lesson we need to learn, He allows those natural consequences—even when it's inconvenient, even when we plead for it to be otherwise—to take their course.

So, think about it . . .

What corrupt apps have you installed in your life? Things you've let in that weren't part of you when you were born? What things are creating interference and keeping you from hearing or feeling the Spirit in your life? The longer you live with them, the shorter the time between the "crashes," and the longer the time you will go without the personal revelation you so desperately need in your life.

Is it time to uninstall?

Some apps are dangerous because they can cause interference . . . and frustration . . . and discouragement . . . so that we can't hear what God is trying to tell us through the Spirit. And so, just like we choose to install those things in our lives, we have to choose to uninstall them too. Repent and remove any interference between you and the Spirit, and you'll be amazed at how much easier it is to feel and hear the Spirit in your life.

Taking Up Your Sword

While putting on the whole armor of God will protect you in the battle of life, the *sword of the Spirit* is what you will have to defend yourself in battle. And why on earth would you want to go into any battle without the ability to defend yourself? You wouldn't. And you don't have to. Your Father in Heaven has given you the opportunity to dress yourself in every bit of armor you need to do everything He needs you to do in this life. Taking up your sword is a critical piece of that armor. Now that you know what that sword really is, do everything in your power to sharpen it and keep it close. Never leave your house without the *sword of the Spirit*.

Armor Up!

Here are five things you can do to take up your sword. We invite you to take at least one (and hopefully all five) of these invitations:

1. *Always* have the sword of the Spirit with you to *guide, guard,* and *heal* you. Always.

2. Learn *how* the Spirit speaks to *you.* Take up the sword of the Spirit like you would take up a language: practice it, practice it, practice it, until you find the most natural grip on the Holy Ghost for you.

3. Start living "as if." Wake up tomorrow and *expect* revelations, as if the Holy Ghost will guide you tomorrow. He will if we look for Him and let Him.

4. Give the Spirit opportunities. Find your place that's easiest for the Spirit to talk to you directly.

5. Remove interference. Through sincere repentance, uninstall those third-party apps that are inconsistent with your spiritual operating system.

Continue the Conversation . . .

Laurel Christensen wrote that the Spirit speaks to individuals in different ways. In this roundtable discussion at seek .deseretbook.com/armorup, the authors share how the Spirit speaks to them. You may find it worthwhile to see what exactly is different and what is similar about some of their responses.

 At seek.deseretbook.com/armorup, click on Roundtable Discussions to follow the authors' roundtable discussion for this chapter.

CONCLUSION

Putting on the armor of God comes line upon line, a little at a time. As you've read this book you've been invited to "Armor Up" by *doing* things in your life that will help you to "put on the whole armor of God, that ye may be able to stand against the wiles of the devil" (Ephesians 6:11). As you take these invitations and *do* things in your life to put on the armor of God you will, slowly but surely, feel the power of the armor of God in your life.

Elder M. Russell Ballard used this analogy: "I like to think of this spiritual armor not as a solid piece of metal molded to fit the body, but more like chain mail. Chain mail consists of dozens of tiny pieces of steel fastened together to allow the user greater flexibility without losing protection. I say that because it has been my experience, covering many more years than you have yet been privileged to live, that there is not one great and grand thing we can do to arm ourselves spiritually. True spiritual power lies in numerous smaller acts woven together in a fabric of spiritual fortification that protects and shields from all evil."[1]

The "small and simple" acts you make to put on the armor of God will bring about "great things" in your life (see Alma 37:6). After teaching about the armor of God, the Lord gave this promise: "Be faithful until I come, and ye shall be caught up, that where I am ye shall be also" (D&C 27:18). This promise is yours, as you faithfully wear the armor of God.

We'll leave you with one more (short) video to watch from Elder Dallin H. Oaks. Armor up!
http://www.lds.org/media-library/video/doctrine-and
-covenants-visual-resources?lang=eng&start=61&
end=72#2010-07-030-take-upon-you-my-whole-armor

NOTES

Chapter One: Girt About with Truth

1. Boyd K. Packer, "Little Children," *Ensign*, November 1986, 17.

2. See Laura Bell, "Let's Talk About Sex," *Reader's Digest*, March 2008.

3. Spencer W. Kimball, "Guidelines to Carry Forth the Work of God in Cleanliness," *Ensign*, May 1974, 7; citing Billy Graham, "What the Bible Says About Sex," *Reader's Digest*, May 1970, 118.

4. Bruce C. and Marie K. Hafen, "'Bridle All Your Passions,'" *Ensign*, February 1994, 15.

5. Truman G. Madsen, *The Temple: Where Heaven Meets Earth* (Salt Lake City: Deseret Book, 2008), 21.

6. See Lawrence B. Finer, "Trends in Premarital Sex in the United States, 1954–2003," *Public Health Reports*, January/February 2007.

7. See Dean M. Busby, et al., "Compatibility or restraint? The effects of sexual timing on marriage relationships," *Journal of Family Psychology*, 24(6): 2010.

8. See Kaye Wellings, et al., "Sexual Behaviour in Context: A Global Perspective," *The Lancet*, November 2006.

9. Elaine S. Dalton, *Return to Virtue* (Salt Lake City: Deseret Book, 2011), 73.

Chapter Two: A Bulletproof Breastplate

1. See http://www.pbs.org/wgbh/nova/heart/heartfacts.html; accessed 13 October 2012.

2. Henry B. Eyring, "We Must Raise Our Sights," *Ensign*, September 2004, 16.

3. Ibid., 16–17.

4. Ezra Taft Benson, "A Mighty Change of Heart," *Ensign*, October 1989, 5.

5. "Entertainment and Media," *For the Strength of Youth* (Salt Lake City: The Church of Jesus Christ of Latter-day Saints, 2011), 11; available at https://www.lds.org/youth/for_the_strength_of_youth?lang=eng; accessed 13 October 2012.

6. Ibid., 12–13.

7. David A. Bednar, Brigham Young University–Idaho devotional, 6 January 2004, available at http://www2.byui.edu/Presentations /transcripts/devotionals/2004_01_06_bednar.htm; accessed 13 October 2012.

8. David A. Bednar, "Seek Learning by Faith," *Ensign*, September 2007, 64.

9. Neil L. Andersen, "Repent . . . That I May Heal You," *Ensign*, November 2009, 41.

Chapter Three: Put On Your Gospel Shoes

1. See http://www.happyworker.com/magazine/weird/fab-foot-facts-and -statistics; accessed 13 October 2012.

2. See http://www.definitions.net/definition/shod; accessed 13 October 2012.

3. See Bible Dictionary, s.v. "Grace," 697.

4. "Go Forward with Faith," *For the Strength of Youth* (Salt Lake City: The Church of Jesus Christ of Latter-day Saints, 2011), 43; available at https://www.lds.org/youth/for-the-strength-of-youth/go-forward -with-faith?lang=eng; accessed 13 October 2012.

5. See Walter Kirn, "Mormons Rock" *Newsweek*, June 2011; available at http://www.thedailybeast.com/newsweek/2011/06/05/mormons -rock.html; accessed 13 October 2012.

Chapter Four: Shields Up!

1. Vaughn J. Featherstone, "The Torchbearer," Brigham Young University Fireside, 5 June 1983, in *Brigham Young University 1982– 83 Fireside and Devotional Speeches* (Provo, UT: Brigham Young University Press, 1983), 145.

2. Marion D. Hanks, *Make It a Good Day*, Brigham Young University Speeches of the Year, 27 September 1966, audiocassette (Provo, UT: Brigham Young University Media Services, 1966).

3. Boyd K. Packer, "How to Survive in Enemy Territory," Seminary Centennial Broadcast, 2012; available at https://www.lds.org /broadcasts/article/seminary-centennial-broadcast/2012/02/how-to -survive-in-enemy-territory?lang=eng; accessed 12 November 2012.

4. Henry B. Eyring, "O Remember, Remember," *Ensign*, November 2007, 67.

5. "Count Your Blessings," *Hymns of The Church of Jesus Christ of Latter-day Saints* (Salt Lake City: The Church of Jesus Christ of Latter-day Saints, 1985), no. 241.

6. "How Firm a Foundation," *Hymns*, no. 85.

7. Bruce C. Hafen, *Spiritually Anchored in Unsettled Times* (Salt Lake City: Deseret Book, 2009), 33.

8. Boyd K. Packer, quoted in Gerry Avant, "'There is no fear in the work we do,' says Pres. Packer," *Church News*, 3 March 2012; available at http://www.ldschurchnews.com/articles/62078/There-is-no-fear-in -the-work-we-do-says-Pres-Packer.html; accessed 13 October 2012.

Chapter Five: Buckle On Your Helmet

1. James E. Faust, "Keep Your Chin Strap Fastened," *New Era*, November 1981, 4.

2. Gordon B. Hinckley, "The Body Is Sacred," *New Era*, November 2006, 2.

3. Gordon B. Hinckley, "The Scourge of Illicit Drugs," *Ensign*, November 1989, 50.

4. "Physical and Emotional Health," *For the Strength of Youth* (Salt Lake City: The Church of Jesus Christ of Latter-day Saints, 2011), 26–27; available at https://www.lds.org/youth/for-the-strength-of -youth?lang=eng; accessed 13 October 2012.

5. Dallin H. Oaks, "Pornography," *Ensign*, May 2005, 88.

6. "Entertainment and Media," *For the Strength of Youth* (Salt Lake City: The Church of Jesus Christ of Latter-day Saints, 2011), 12; available at https://www.lds.org/youth/for-the-strength-of-youth?lang=eng; accessed 13 October 2012.

7. Jeffrey R. Holland, "Place No More for the Enemy of My Soul," *Ensign*, May 2010, 44.

Chapter Six: Your Spiritual Sword

1. "Let the Holy Spirit Guide," *Hymns of The Church of Jesus Christ of Latter-day Saints* (Salt Lake City: The Church of Jesus Christ of Latter-day Saints, 1985), no. 143.

2. Brigham Young, *Discourses of Brigham Young*, comp. John A. Widtsoe (Salt Lake City: Deseret Book, 1999), 33.

3. Neal A. Maxwell, "Revelation," *First Worldwide Leadership Training Meeting*, 11 January 2003, 5.

4. Joseph Smith, *History of The Church of Jesus Christ of Latter-day Saints*, 7 vols., edited by B. H. Roberts (Salt Lake City: The Church of Jesus Christ of Latter-day Saints, 1932–51), 6:58.

Conclusion

1. M. Russell Ballard, "Be Strong in the Lord, and in the Power of His Might," Brigham Young University fireside, 3 March 2002; available at http://speeches.byu.edu/reader/reader.php?id=613; accessed 13 October 2012.

ABOUT THE
AUTHORS

John Bytheway may own every Star Trek movie ever made, but he insists he gave away all his action figures. He served a mission to the Philippines and later graduated from Brigham Young University. He is the author of many best-selling books, audio talks, and DVDs. He and his wife, Kimberly, have six children. Visit John on Facebook.

Laurel Christensen spends the majority of her summers speaking at girls' camps all across the country and loves it. She is the author of *He Loves Us and We Love Him*, a book celebrating the Young Women theme. You can find her on Facebook or e-mail her at Laurel.Christensen@gmail.com.

John Hilton III loves being with the youth of the church! He and his wife, Lani Hilton, are the parents of five children and co-authors of *What Guys Need to Know about Girls / What Girls Need to Know about Guys*. For more information, please visit johnhiltoniii.com.

Hank Smith and his wife, Sara, both grew up in St. George, Utah. They are the parents of five children (including brand-new twin boys!). Hank is the author of many talks on CD, including *Thou Shalt Be Nice*, *Break Up with the World*, and *5 Temptation Killers*. Come chat with Hank at www.facebook .com/hanksmithcds.

Anthony Sweat teaches the gospel to youth and young adults for his profession. He is the author of *Mormons: An Open Book*. He is married to the lovely Cindy Sweat and they are the parents of six children. For more information, please visit anthony sweat.com.

Brad Wilcox and his wife have four children and three grand-children. He loves teaching at BYU, speaking to the youth, and writing. He doesn't love exercise, but he is trying hard to have a better attitude. He recently ran his first half-marathon (and lived to tell about it). Visit Brad at bradwilcox.com.